TWELVE PRINCIPLES

12
TWELVE PRINCIPLES

for a successful co-operation between childcare workers and parents

Roger Prott/Annette Hautumm

uitgeverij
SWP

This publication was supported by a financial contribution of the Bernard van Leer Foundation, The Hague, The Netherlands.

Original title:
12 Prinzipien für eine erfolgreiche Zusammenarbeit von Erzieherinnen und Eltern
Roger Prott & Annette Hautumm
ISBN 3 937785 01 9

Twelve principles
for a successful co-operation between childcare workers and parents
Roger Prott & Annette Hautumm

ISBN 90 6665 618 2
NUR 742

OVERVIEW

PRELIMINARY NOTE

Parents are the first and, in the majority of cases, the most important people in the first years of a child's development. Additionally, the child establishes relations with other people – children as well as adults. Some of these grown-ups get into touch with the children for professional reasons. Throughout this brochure they will collectively be referred to as *childcare workers*. They are in charge of early childhood support. In addition to the home setting, they care for the child, they raise and educate him/her during specific times of the day.

Undoubtedly, a basic agreement between the childcare workers and the parents on the goals and values is of great benefit to the children's development, whereas (untreated) tensions and different ideas about the principles of support turn out disadvantageous for the children. In this context it is of little importance whether the differences clearly show or remain hidden in mutual ignorance. What counts for the children is the adults' basic mutual acceptance even of different actions, as long as these can be clearly assigned to and do not impose loyalty conflicts on them. Children are by all means able to accept and handle varying patterns of behaviour of their parents, grandparents or even the childcare worker respectively. However, they will definitely suffer if the differences become contradictory in the end.

Since it is the childcare worker's task to support the children by offering group-activities, it is necessary that parents basically agree to her[1] work, so that the children will not be faced with such conflicts. Moreover, she must understand that none of her pedagogical efforts will turn out successful if it does not comply with the parents' will. This explains why her professional work and her strive for success call for co-ordination with the parents.

Co-ordinating the different ideas requires regular contacts between the childcare worker and the parents in childcare centres[2]. As far as I know, this view has become widely accepted too. However, there exist manifold ideas about the regularity and the content of these contacts. They vary according to the cultural traditions, the childcare workers' respective tasks, or the opportunities available in everyday practice. The necessity to co-ordinate the basic ideas shared by childcare workers and parents calls for co-operation. Along with the claim for mutual acceptance, this idea culminates in the demand for a *partnership* between the childcare workers and the parents – which, I am afraid, is extremely difficult to realise in many a place.

Over the years

In everyday practice of both groups, the childcare workers in the childcare centres and the parents, the mutual contacts may bring about insecurity, anxiety, disappointment and fear, but also delight, appreciation and success. During my professional training as a early childhood pedagogue, I came to understand that *working together with the parents (parent project)* is part of the professional performance. It

1 Tribute is paid to the female profession of childcare workers by applying 'she' or 'her' respectively throughout this brochure.

2 In the following, this expression is used for all institutionalised forms of early childhood support whose qualified professional staff work with the children in addition to family-style parenting.

was basically understood as organising parents' evenings whose topics would depend on the problems that had been identified by the professional staff. Most popular were those topics:

- that were rooted in a (latent) conflict with a single child's parents (in order to avoid direct confrontation, this was introduced however to all parents as a subject of general interest);
- that focused on children's deviant behaviour;
- that called on the parents indirectly to better adjust their family-style parenting to the education as practised in the childcare centre, since its staff after all, due to their expertise, knew best what to do.

Further popular topics following this line were 'the deviant child', 'consistent education', 'responsibility and security', 'getting prepared for school', or 'punishment and education'. During the times when parents would bring or pick up their children, hurried informal exchange about the most important daily incidents was also part of the *parent project*. Sometimes I wonder whether this form of communication was purposefully invented to conceal that parents were forbidden admission to the group-rooms.

This presentation seems only exaggerated in its résumé. I would like to emphasise that at the time we always understood ourselves as the parents' supporters – even their partners – eager to achieve the best possible for each individual child. Therefore we turned to reading books and to attending advanced training courses to learn about additional forms of the *parent project* or collect tips for a more attractive organisation of parents' evenings. We considered the broadcasting-times of football matches, so that the fathers would not stay away. We discussed, whether beer or wine could be tolerated or tea, water and juices only. Casual sitting-corners, chairs for adults, seasonal room decorations, scheduling, this and much more was and still is being taken into account wherever *co-operation with the parents* or *partnership* is spoken or written about.

At the time, I was not aware that organisational issues need clarifying and that planning and arranging the parents' evenings must be carefully considered; but, above all that professional childcare workers need to adopt a different attitude if they really wish to get through to the parents. Only later I came to realise that my expertise concerning educational processes was different but by no means more valuable.
As an amateur film maker, it was fairly easy for me to record the children and the daily routine of the institution, which I did first just for the fun of it. Later I showed the pictures to the parents. Still, it was not technology that fascinated the parents most, but rather their children as well as the transparency of the pedagogical work.

Later I learnt that parents and childcare workers also need to further specify the seemingly obvious basis of their meetings. Vague ideas on it can cause a lot of misunderstandings. Moreover, a clear distinction between the basic conditions and the goals must be made. Then it will be possible to recognise that for example 'confidence among adults', as a rule, can only develop by sharing the same experiences, otherwise it is nothing but an idealistic obligation. 'Have confidence!' is an encouragement which seems as impossible to realise as 'Be spontaneous!' The conscious overcoming of fear or distrust alone does not lead to confidence necessarily.

An assignment

Nowadays I work as a freelance consultant in the field of 'early childhood support in childcare centres'. So I was asked by the Bernard-van-Leer-Foundation in The Hague/The Netherlands to hold a short introductory lecture on 'Partnership between childcare workers and parents' on the fourth Central and Eastern European Early Childhood Care and Development Regional Meeting (CEEECCD) in Belgrade 2002. Only gradually did I realise what my assent really meant. With view to the variety of participating states, whose conditions I was not at all familiar with, something had to be discovered that all of them shared, something that would be accepted, arouse interest and get things ahead.

Thus the idea originated to develop principles that would support the childcare workers in establishing *partnership* with the parents, regardless of national borders and cultures. Since it was obvious that mainly experts would participate in the conference, I tried to adopt their positions. Very soon questions came up: What does *partnership* mean within this framework? What kind of partners are parents and childcare workers? Are they to behave like business partners? Certainly they should act professionally, but business-minded – no, thank you. Should they act like sparring partners? In this case, one of the participants was bound to become the champion, easily knocking out his/her training partner. That would also show a misleading picture. Do parents and childcare workers bear close relationships with one another? No, they need not love each other, but... yes, they should co-operate!

The idea was born that the best co-operation possible is more crucial for the childcare workers and the parents than partnership is. Additionally, no decision for or against either side had to be made. It was rather a question of what to focus on or which priorities to establish, which is a precondition for co-operation and (perhaps) future partnership.

The participants' reactions at the conference showed that a further aspect had come to the fore: the need to discharge the relations between parents and childcare workers from overabundant moral-laden demands. A certain disillusionment was spreading, but at the same time also the insight that co-operation between the parents and the childcare workers as such is difficult enough to achieve – and this is true of the majority of the participating countries.

The principles

In this context, I understand principles as general rules or fundamentals for facilitating target-oriented activities. The principles must comply with the respective goals and not contradict them. They are meant to serve as benchmarks by which one's own specific activities can be measured.

The quoted principles, with one exception, are phrased as suggestions for the childcare workers and their activities. They are my foremost addressees. It is not at all disadvantageous if the parents and the responsible bodies of childcare centres know these principles and, together with *their* childcare workers, will come to a joint agreement on how this will affect their specific co-operation. The principles may serve as guide-lines for the childcare worker's tasks, but they cannot replace them. The aim is to achieve the best possible form of co-operation. The principles should support the childcare workers in their interaction with the parents.

In each single case, our considerations will refer to a situation where parents send their children into childcare centres funded by private or public bodies. I assume that the principles can be applied on either type. Parent-run institutions, with parents employing childcare workers, will not be separately discussed in this context.

The publication

The text is divided into three parts. Ideas, representing a contextual linkage to the principles subsumed, will come first. Although the principles follow a specific sequence, they, or the respective paragraphs, can be read and worked on independently. Each principle will be explained according to the set frame. Positions up to discussion and examples are collected in separate boxes. Some terms will be spelt *in italics*, like *co-operation* and *partnership*, because they require particular attention. Although they are used quite naturally in daily practice, it happens easily that they are assigned different meanings. It is important for the communicating partners to establish an unequivocal common understanding of these terms.

In the meantime, two extra principles have been added to the ten original ones, since, after the conference, the Bernard-van-Leer Foundation asked for an extended version. The original character of the principles was largely to be maintained: short, precise, stimulating further discussions. Therefore, this text can neither be compared with a manual about *the co-operation between childcare workers and parents,* nor does it offer detailed instructions on how to proceed.
Stylistically, the first person mode is used throughout this brochure in order to keep up the same personal form of address as in the lecture. This mode does by no means underrate Ms Annette Hautumm's contributions. Without her stimulating ideas and critical comments this current version could not have been realised.

Roger Prott
Berlijn, February 2004

1

PART ONE
preconditions for co-operation

The way to *co-operation* resembles rather a steep and stony mountain trail than a smooth motorway in the plains.

The foundation of a house is crucial for its future size, its ground plan and its usage. It is essential for the stability of the house. Before working on the foundation, various preconditions need to be settled: for example, whether there is muddy or rocky ground, who will be in charge of the construction management, how the remaining work will be divided, which purpose the house will serve in future and who will provide overall financing.

It is a process similar to the relationship between the childcare workers and the parents in childcare centres. Sound relations can neither be claimed or prescribed, nor explained one-sidedly. Good relations – however this may be understood – are perceived as such by both sides. They develop gradually. Or rather: good relations form step by step. Having settled the preconditions, the fundation can be worked on. In each phase, the working process and the respective current achievements must be secured.

The first five principles help to clarify the preconditions for the quality of the relationship between the childcare workers and the parents. Along with its documentation, one working-result becomes obvious at the very beginning of the text. The chapter is titled *preconditions for co-operation*, which means that the first principle was applied and that I have already made an important decision. *Partnership* between childcare workers and parents is not my first goal. Instead, I am struggling for a qualified *co-operation* between them. For you, dear readers, this decision is still to be taken. It will contribute to orientation, thereby helping to avoid errors and misunderstandings which may result from demanding too much. *Co-operation* first, partnership (perhaps) later!

The following three principles emphasise the institutional preconditions for *co-operation*. Since, apart from the interests of the groups involved, the circumstances of the relevant child-supporting institutions must be considered. Not every childcare centre is provided with the same or unequivocal job-assignment. Occasionally, good intentions of the people involved in the childcare scheme cannot fully develop, because the childcare workers fail to sufficiently consider that parents perceive them not only as individuals but also as members of an institutional authority (principle 4) and consequently as representatives of a professionally-legitimised power (principle 5). Parents are not able to take up contact with the childcare worker without reservations.

Childcare workers and parents come together in the childcare centre. None of them really feels at home there, but all the same, there exist clear domestic authorisations. What may the landlords (hosts) tell the guests without being impolite? What must be observed by the guests? The diversity of cultural traditions imposes different rights and duties on both groups, hosts and guests alike. In one place, the host must share everything, in another place the guest must decline over and over what is being offered. Elsewhere the guests will be offered the most comfortable bed, and in another area they have to prove their politeness by showing absolute reservation. Who is allowed to utter wishes? Are all people involved aware of the expectations towards one another resulting from their respective cultural backgrounds? What can be taken for granted? Paying attention to these considerations is already hard to do in the familiar circumstances of privacy. An institutional framework, in which childcare workers are no hosts and parents are no guests (or should not be), calls for particular caution. These relationships will become even more difficult to understand, when people from different cultural backgrounds meet.

Superficially, everything looks fairly easy. It seems as if people meet who would only need to respect and appreciate one another and socialise in an open relationship. Unfortunately, life is not that easy. A lot of publications number respect, appreciation and open-mindedness as preconditions for the *co-operation* between childcare workers and parents. They do not appear in this text, since I do not consider them preconditions. Respect, appreciation and open-mindedness result from experiences. At best they are interim goals on the way to *co-operation*, if not even its indicators only.

PRINCIPLE

1 2 3 4 5 6
7 8 9 10 11 12

Find out about your understanding of *co-operation* and *partnership* and what you are really striving for!

With the first principle I would like to refer to the goal of all collective efforts. When taking action, goals can be compared to lighthouses which everybody wants to get at. Therefore it is necessary to define an as clearly as possible goal and to explain it.

This principle implies that the predominant goal has not been decided on yet. Possibly, such important issues leave only little or no room at all for the childcare workers' own decision making. Even under these circumstances, further clarification is still required.

It must also be questioned, whether you and the responsible body of the institution share the same view (see principle 3) – a process similar to the way you are handling the paper at hand.

What are you, the childcare worker, trying to achieve in your relationship with and together with the parents?
Are you willing to co-operate with the parents?
If so, which tasks shall be tackled?
How shall the division of labour be organised?
Are you interested in becoming the parents' partner?
Shall the parents become your partners?
Are you rather thinking of a game, a life, or a business related partnership?

Do you imagine a junior and a senior partner?
How will the shares in the business be split up?

I am struggling for *co-operation between childcare workers and parents*. In the following, I will explain why.
Making a distinction between *partnership* and *co-operation* is already important, because these terms imply different assumptions on how and why parents and childcare workers (should) cope with one another. Partners can co-operate. But in order to do so, nobody needs to join a partnership. *Co-operation* and *partnership* describe interpersonal relations in different ways.
The concept of *partnership* emphasises the relationship between the two adult groups who are involved in the childcare scheme in childcare centres. Childcare workers and parents are expected to consider each other partners and to act accordingly, for instance by:

- dealing fairly with one another;
- trusting each other;
- becoming aware of their joint responsibility.

The abstract term of *partner(ship)* is defined by the three above listed notions fairness, trust, and responsibility. Does this offer better orientation? Rather not, because these terms are abstract, too. They require interpretation and communication. In a way, they even complicate the struggle for *partnership*, because fairness, trust, and responsibility are highly moral-laden values. They cannot really be questioned:

- May a person admit that he/she prefers to behave unfairly once in a while?
- Who would seriously question the value of shared responsibility?
- Who has the courage to admit that his or her confidence is only poorly developed?

- Is a person able to disclose this shortcoming, or does admitting it require the very confidence that is in fact missing?

Who is propagating the concept of *partnership* and why? Parents are 'the parents of ...' Or they introduce themselves as 'Mr and Mrs ...' They do not speak of themselves as 'the child-care workers' partners', quite opposite to the professional assistants and consultants who are only too keen on adopting the roles of 'the parents' partners'.

Specialists as professional assistants share the joint obligation to achieve something together with or via the parents. They know that their work will become more efficient if they succeed in gaining the parents' confidence. Therefore a lot of experts are eager to become partners and, in order to be on the safe side, to upgrade their complete work-liaison to *partnership*. Partners should trust each other, shouldn't they? They forget that trust needs to grow first. At the same time they fail to remember that each single, even hidden demand for trust arouses suspicion.

For this reason I seriously doubt that this approach will lead to the hoped-for success. It is notably threatened by covert demands, unsettled preconditions, and a lot of topics in need of further explanations – altogether issues that release misunderstandings, thereby becoming obstacles on the stony path towards *partnership*.

In my opinion, this concept conceals a longing for harmony, for agreeable social conduct and assistance. This desire, which seems kind of interwoven with *partnership*, becomes disadvantageous if it remains hidden, because it calls for something that will only slowly grow – sometimes by way of disharmonious conflicts. Moreover, the desire draws the attention away from one's own scope of activities.

The concept of *co-operation* between childcare workers and parents seems to me a more promising approach to the work in childcare centres. Its name speaks for itself: Joint efforts! Although far from being a magic formula, it offers a lot of chances and a broad range of possible independent activities for childcare workers as well as parents.

The concept of *co-operation* makes target-oriented activities and agreements possible. *Co-operation* comprises both – new ways as well as failures. Whereas setbacks in the concept of *partnership* are instantly attributed to a lack of responsibility or the betrayal of trust – in other words to grave crises in the partnership –, errors in the concept of *co-operation* offer new opportunities of joint efforts. Failures bring about as much benefit as success does.

The concept of *co-operation* offers the possibility of self-determined achievable goals. Together, childcare workers and parents can define the tasks they are to work on both independently and together with a view on a single or on several goals. Success is not taken for granted. All the same, positive results show at any intermediate stage, not only at the end of a long process. *Co-operation* provides the chance of evaluating each single work-result positively.

Even supposed minor achievements mean progress. Each person involved can and may contribute as much as possible according to one's current individual potentials and interests.

Co-operation between childcare workers and parents can take place anywhere and in manifold ways. Both minor and major contributions are possible. There exist numerous attempts of measuring and evaluating the quality of co-operation. Anyone interested in doing so may carry on. Apart from that, it is the co-operating people who really count. Do they accept the working process and its outcome and how long will they be satisfied with it?

However, the chief attraction of the concept of *co-operation* between the childcare workers and the parents is the possibility of real *partnership* in the end. If *partnership* is relieved of its moralising share, it may well be defined as a form of highly developed co-operation

- with goals that have collectively been worked out and confirmed by all people involved;
- that needs a lot of time and energy to develop;
- that is based on quite a number of collective experiences;
- that calls for a securing framework;
- that acknowledges all shares as equal;
- and that is founded on equal rights of all people involved.

Trust evolves from experience. *Co-operation* means shared experience. Trust stands at the end of a multi-faceted developmental process that childcare workers and parents have to go through. This process can be regarded as being accomplished once the participants have developed enough confidence to act as independent co-operating partners.

Check whether the interests of the stakeholders immediately concerned — the childcare centre, the parents and the institution — really meet!

Childcare workers and parents are said to share interests. I do not take this for granted, but all the same I still consider it possible. In childcare institutions, the childcare workers and the parents meet for two comparable reasons. They expect the children to become supported and cared for in the centre, so that they themselves can earn their living.
For the childcare workers, the first motive of childminding coincides with the second one, because it constitutes their profession. The parents, on the other hand, must leave their children when they go to work.[1]

What are your interests as a childcare worker?
Are you looking forward to working together with the children according to your ideas? Does the children's affection make you feel good?
Being an expert, do you need the parents' appreciation?
Do you think society should provide more means for early childhood support?

Which of the parents' ideas are you familiar with?

---

[1] Not taking into account the situation in which parents who are not employed send their children into day-care too.

Which do you assume?
Do the parents show relief when their children are handed over to them safe and sound?
Do they wish to be informed about the daily events or do they confide in the professional without questioning?
Are the parents interested in their children's developmental progress?
Are they actively involved in improving the general conditions?

What kind of policies is your institution/organisation pursuing?
Is a specific pedagogical concept being supported by the responsible body?
Are pedagogical goals dominated by security regulations?
Is the quality of the institution being monitored? If so, how is it done?
Are parents intruding into the course of events if they want to contribute more than their usual parental activities?
Is the parents' co-operation being promoted? If so, how and why?

Childcare workers and parents can pursue different and even contradictory interests. A conflict of interests often stems from different ideas about childminding, but there are also other reasons, either rooted in the childcare worker's profession or set by the institution.

Children shall be 'well supported and cared for' in the centres. Does this mean they need a lot of stimulation by the childcare workers and only little room for their own self-determined activities? Or vice versa? Supposing the children are very busy playing with each other, would parents possibly think that the children are left to themselves? In this case, parents will ask for 'more support'. In their view, this means asking for 'the childcare worker's increased efforts', whereas she on her part would probably prefer maintaining an even lower profile.

This example refers to different attitudes of the childcare worker and the parents towards the pedagogical task and shows that the parents' critical review of both the pedagogical approach as such and the childcare worker's performance come very close. The two aspects need to be distinctly kept apart, thereby easing communication.

However, this example is a bit more complicated, because the interests underlying the different attitudes concerning pedagogics and the necessary work performance have not been mentioned so far. In this case, the childcare worker's and the parents' interests may even be identical – such as achieving the best possible support for the children – and still conflicts may arise. Actually, it happens very seldomly that shared interests clearly show. If the issues of joint efforts are not resolved, conflicts are more likely to come up.

In addition, identical interests may stem from different motives. Provided the motives are too much focused on and become the main objects of conflicts, differences instead of joint efforts will come to the fore. If, as the above mentioned example shows, childcare workers and parents have claimed the best possible support for the children as their common interest, the childcare worker's motive may be to improve her professional prestige or to safeguard her job. The parents' interests for example may show in exaggerated demands for pedagogical support for their child, caused by the motives of ambition, fear or ignorance. The motives on either side cannot be negotiated against each other. Childcare workers and parents should accept them as a matter of fact and concentrate on what they are able to collectively achieve.

Physicians and lawyers enjoy high professional prestige. Their vocational training takes place on an advanced level, their lobbies protect professional interests against the outside and control quality inside, their pay is more than average. An occupation is considered professional if it has become so specialised that virtually no outside observer is able to understand the fundamentals. Obviously, laymen and professionals must be strictly distinguished.

In comparison, childcare workers are in a difficult position. They must learn to accept that other people know something about education too or at least believe to do so – this applies the more, the younger the children are. This explains why child rearing in day-care is generally considered an occupation with only (too) little professionalism and (too) low a profile. This situation clearly shows and results in the fact that it is mainly women who are employed in day-care.

Improving their job profile is one of the childcare workers' professional interests. Therefore they might be tempted to follow a model of professionalism which works successfully with other occupations but cannot be applied to pedagogical work. If, for example, childcare workers try to use their expertise for marking off their own professional guild, they in fact exclude those parents who they are actually to co-operate with, because otherwise they will not be able to fulfil their tasks at the required quality level (see principle 6). Different professional interests will lead to conflict-ridden situations in this case. They may be reinforced if a childcare worker is faced with parents who are willing to participate in a childcare centre's activities by providing their own ideas and concepts, whereas the childcare worker feels (still) insecure and controlled. She will first of all have to bring herself to offer the parents direct access to her work.

Some parents do in fact want to keep an eye on the childcare worker, because they are afraid that they are losing control over their child's upbringing. Although this may complicate the handling of the parents, it shows at the same time that parents are interested in their child. They are not indifferent towards their child. Other parents feel perfectly fine if (or although) they are not involved in their child's support in day-care. Still, it does not necessarily mean that they are indifferent towards their child's development. In their view, this attitude may even express trust in the childcare worker and her ability to offer good quality education and care.

Almost any form of parental behaviour can be interpreted in different ways. Which is the correct one? What are the parents' interests and motives? A person who is not familiar with them will not be able to check whether they meet his or her own interests.

Childcare centres are institutions (see principle 4). It is typical for institutions that they develop their own interests, which sometimes run counter to their assignment. Some of them, for instance, are only open for people entitled. Although visitors are welcome occasionally, they are accepted, above all, for handing over and picking up those attending. Consequently, schools and hospitals serve as institutionalised models for childcare centres. Only recently has it become accepted that even in this context parents play an important role in the development of their children. However, this knowledge has not yet become materialised in the form of a systematic co-operation between the staff and the parents.

The more the policy of a childcare centre resembles a traditional school or hospital and the less influence on institutional routine is tolerated, the fewer the chances of (parental) participation and commitment. This may present the perfect childcare organisation according to the ideal shared by the bodies of the institution, the childcare workers and the parents; also, the interests of the three stakeholders can focus on co-operation to a large extent. In both cases serious problems are hardly to be expected. Only when different interests collide, problems are likely to arise.

Supposing that supporting the children and caring for their well-being are matters of shared interest of childcare workers and parents and that this has been recognised and co-ordinated, it does not necessarily result in a task that must be fulfilled together. In any case, childcare workers and parents can pursue their common interests independently and in their own respective area of responsibility. It remains necessary to accept each other's competences and to respect the relevant limits. Under these circumstances it is most probable that everybody involved will be satisfied.

Example: In the everyday practice of the 'École maternelle" in France, practical *co-operation* between the professionals and the parents can only seldomly be found. Parents are at hand only, when they bring their children in the mornings and pick them up when the hours of daycare are over. The *co-operation* between the childcare workers/teachers and the parents is essentially limited to participating in the committees. Since this is a well-functioning system which has become commonly accepted throughout the country, we may conclude that the motives and interests of all stakeholders, that is the parents, the childcare workers and the institution, have become satisfactorily co-ordinated.

PRINCIPLE 1 2 3 4 5 6 7 8 9 10 11 12

Clarify the precise assignment of your institution in order to develop a realistic concept of co-operation!

If you want to find out about the people and their respective interests in childrearing, initiate a discussion on the assignment of your childcare centre! What is it meant for? What is it to achieve? Do all people involved share similar ideas on the purpose of their institution with early childhood support as its first priority? Do the childcare workers, the parents and the bodies understand the same message when the general purpose is explained by way of examples? Do all of them agree? What do people on the outside expect from the organisation?

What shall be offered by the institution?
What kind of expectations shall be met?
Can the full purpose of the centre be derived from its name?
What kind of statements are used by your institution or organisation for advertising campaigns?
What are the parents' expectations like?
What do they pay for?
Who are the main target groups for activities?
Who else, how much should they feel obliged?
What have you, the childcare worker, been prepared and trained for?
What kind of quality-criteria need to be met?

Most children are brought up in their families, there enjoying care and support while growing up. Attending special organisations during certain times of the day additionally, is a supplement to family education. In such places, adults observe that the children are cared for and supported in their development.

For this purpose, organisations have been established with a great variation of policies, general conditions and traditions. Some of them are predominantly focusing on supporting the intellectual development of children. Others concentrate on childcare during the parents' absence. A third group does not make any difference between intellectual education and care. They follow the basic principle that education and care should be considered a single unit. Some organisations have been planned for age-specific groups only, whereas others accept any child of pre-school age (sometimes even beyond school entry). There are organisations which have specialised in supporting children with specific needs and other more comprehensive centres for all children living in the neighbouring area. Childcare organisations can either be exclusively designed for children, or they may be part of another institution, like, for instance, a Maternal Centre, or a state school.

Each type spreads information concerning its predominant ideas about early childhood support, the requested focal points that are being tackled in general, and the specific tasks in particular. Some goals can already be guessed from the kind of organisation. In short, the organisational concept of a childcare centre tells us something about the assignment which it is to fulfil in its respective society or cultural group.

There exist great differences. Safe state funded support serves other purposes than a charity organisation with a minimum scope of supply. In this brochure, although at the cost of simplification, all of these organisations are subsumed under childcare centres, for which the quoted principles are valid under the condition that:

- supporting the children and caring for them is their major assignment;
- they employ specifically trained experts;
- they are to co-operate with the parents of the attending children, so that the assignment of early childhood support can be efficiently put into practice.

With regard to the co-operation between childcare workers and parents, those institutions that, apart from childrearing, also or predominantly focus on the assignment of *parents' education*, will not be considered. The same goes for centres which have specialised in parents' support.

It is important for me to make one more distinction. On the one hand there are centres whose childcare workers can or should co-operate with the parents to achieve the best possible support for the children. On the other hand there are places with childcare workers who are first of all, or additionally, given their own, very special tasks with view to the parents, like for instance offering courses for qualifying parents in educational issues. Undoubtedly, such offers are supportive of the children in the end, but these courses are rather a separate service within the centre's programme than the hoped-for outcome of the child related assignment. In other words: will childcare workers support the attending children's intellectual training and care if they offer information and knowledge to their parents? Or is it the childcare workers' task to qualify all parents, because this approach is considered successful by the social policy of the respective country? Or shall this offer basically be addressed to all adults interested, with the parents of the attending children ranging amongst others?

It is always of vital importance whether parents know what to expect when their child goes into day-care and whether they accept it. Parents who are interested in their child's intellectual support do not necessarily agree to becoming the target group themselves.

It should be emphasised that such targeting interventions must be distinguished from the inevitable process of influencing one another which takes place whenever people get into touch with each other. In this case, parents in childcare centres may benefit from the information about childrearing, psychology, children's stages of development or the family-policy of the respective country. They may qualify themselves that way, but their explicit consent will be needed if they are to additionally become a target group of their own. Everything is settled as long as the parents are clearly expressing their wishes. The parents' consent can also be assumed if they are familiar with the extended assignment of parents' education and thereupon enrol their child in the centre. But also in this case, childcare workers need to be attentive. Possibly, parents and their child have no choice. Therefore they may let themselves in for the offer available but do not really accept it in total.

A similar situation might arise if childcare workers, due to their personal commitment, extend their assignment of child related pedagogical work, because they, quite understandably, realise that some parents are in need of information. This means walking a tightrope. Will the parents gladly welcome this offer, since they did not have the courage to ask for it? Will they be surprised or annoyed for fear of losing face? Will they accept the offer because renouncing it could turn out disadvantageous for their child?

Childcare workers who are struggling for successful *co-operation*, which might lead to future partnership with the parents, should always remember that partners must accept each other the way they are. *Parents' education,* however, implies that parents need to learn something. They are expected to change, while the childcare worker is not. That is the opposite of acceptance and consequently difficult to tolerate.

Additionally, each form of *parents' education* places the childcare workers (at least temporarily) on a higher level. This will affect the *co-operation* with the parents. Under these circumstances *co-operation* cannot possibly be organised as if the two groups involved were on equal footing.

It is more than a coincidence that, in the concepts of *parents' education*, the parents are referred to as target-groups of the respective offers – these terms have purposefully been adopted in this place. Thus, at least linguistically, parents are made to assimilate the role of passive targets. They become addressees of offers which are to supply them with knowledge, information and skills. Parents are degraded to objects 'that' (in this context the neuter form is purposefully used to underline the parents' passiveness), more or less urgently, need additional education. This object status does not match with the goal of co-operation. Therefore caution is called for, because the assignment of child related support cannot simply be extended by the task of parents' education. So, what are your priorities when having to decide for an assignment? What is your childcare centre mainly intended for?

PRINCIPLE

1 2 3 4 5 6
7 8 9 10 11 12

Mind the barrier between the institution and the individual! Childcare workers should anticipate the parents cautiousness or even anxiety due to earlier experiences!

The following lines, which I would like you to pay attention to, are based on an assumption that, although mentioned earlier, has not been explained yet: childcare centres are institutions.

What is true of the childcare centre you are working in?
Is it run by parents, by parents and childcare workers collectively, by a private body or is it a state-organisation?
Does a child's enrolment require laborious procedures and numerous application-forms?
Is everybody admitted anytime; are only all of the parents admitted anytime; or are there special consultation hours for people from outside?
Is the centre closed during specific times with admission on appointment only?
Is there general admission control; are special forms needed?
Are the children handed over at the entrance or in front of the group room?
Are the parents involved in internal events?
Do the children wear their own individual garments, or uniforms, or is clothing provided for by the centre?

For a lot of people administrative authorities and other institutions are connected with unpleasant experiences such as having to wait for hours until it was their turn. They feel treated like objects, because in such places something is assigned to them. Incomprehensible application forms must be filled in. Certain procedures cannot be understood by an outsider and cannot be influenced without running a risk. The applicant is simply informed about the final decisions. People of influence are sitting inside, whereas those outside feel like petitioners. Many people have experienced that school as an educational institution is not asking for their wishes, interests and skills. Authorities and institutions do not perceive them as individuals, but lump them all together instead or at least divide them into groups. For quite a number of people troubles with the Inland Revenue Office, property management, post office or the application for a driving licence have become part of their daily routine. Due to these experiences they tend to believe that institutions have an advantage over them.

Example 1: There is a long tradition in many countries that childcare centres are run like schools. The parents are requested to bring their children in the mornings, but they are not allowed entrance. As a rule, they are kept off from what is going on inside: from their child, the centre's policies or curriculum, and the practice of care and education. Unless parents are very self-reliant, they will not dare ask for more.

Example 2: Quality criteria for childcare centres from Birmingham (England): can the parents be assured that a serious and appropriate response will follow whenever somebody utters discriminating remarks about their child and his/her cultural/ethnical background?

I would like to take up again two examples in order to interpret them according to the fourth principle.

Firstly: are parents given no choice between childcare centres with different policies, is admission to a place in daycare moreover only possible via waiting list and/or does it require much effort, and are the criteria for admission finally not transparent enough or hardly understandable? If so, parents will come across a lot of obstacles between the childcare worker and themselves. The easier the conditions of admission the more plausible the invitation to co-operation.

Secondly: if childcare workers accept an assignment of *parents' education*, they will adopt the role of the parents' teachers, thereby positioning themselves on a superior level. The basis of co-operation changes. Moreover, parents are likely to remember their experiences during their schooltime. Even though these might have been pleasant, (some) parents will possibly feel like small and dependent pupils again.

For almost any experience there is a new, more agreeable and better substitute. On entering a childcare centre, parents will definitely be influenced by their previous experiences with institutions but hardly ever by prejudices. If everything is organised different from what they have been used to so far, they will find their individual access, if wanted, by undertaking various single steps, and they will develop trust in order to participate. Still, even if they are keen on taking part, a lot of work is left to the childcare workers until parents feel comfortable enough to master their insecurities and thus become actively involved. Parents will always feel most disturbed by the idea that their undoubtedly well-meaning commitment is possibly not appreciated by the childcare workers and might turn out disadvantageous for their child. This idea is omnipresent with all parents as long as they do not develop sufficient trust in the childcare workers. It affects co-operation to a large extent and for a longer period of time.

Parents need to go through a lot of new experiences before they are able to clearly distinguish between the respective shares of the individual childcare worker on the one hand and the institution on the other in the proceedings of the childcare centre. Very soon they will come to appreciate the childcare worker's expertise. Basically they are prepared to inform the childcare worker about their child's behaviour in the home setting, but they are still observing how she is handling such information within the framework of her institution.

With this process under way, an important condition has already been established. Parents will then be enabled to perceive the childcare worker not only as the institution's representative but increasingly as a person by all means able to act individually. The same is valid for the childcare workers. They must realise that meeting the parents means a confrontation of individuals, formed by specific, often negative previous experiences with institutions. Therefore childcare workers have to stand a certain initial reservation on the parents' part. By creating appropriate opportunities, childcare workers must enable the parents to go through (new) experiences. They have to adopt the parents' position, seeing them as individuals and not as a group in which differences can hardly be made out. Consequently, it is necessary for the childcare workers, just like for the parents, to become aware of the individual as well as the institutional character of their encounter. Beforehand, though, they must come to accept the initial situation. When childcare workers and parents come together in a childcare centre, professionals as an institution's representatives meet individuals who are also concerned with childrearing. The complicated wording already shows how much effort is needed before co-operation between childcare workers and parents is actually achieved. The relations between the two sides cannot simply be compared to the casual get-together of guests who happen to meet at the same party.

Perhaps the following idea will help to effectively handle a difficult situation:

Childcare workers should be aware that whenever parents enter a childcare centre, an extraordinary encounter, that is an encounter of two different cultures, takes place.

This sentence considered, parents can be seen from a different angle. Having just been characterised as individuals, they are now attributed a function. They enter the childcare centre as representatives of a different culture. In other words: they represent another institution, because this is what *family* is referred to in other contexts. They deserve the respect that their role requires.

The quality of the co-operation between childcare workers and parents cannot be higher than the respect and appreciation which both sides as representatives of their respective cultures are showing for each other.

PRINCIPLE 1 2 3 4 5 6 7 8 9 10 11 12

Take into consideration that the parents have met many well-meaning consultants and their well-intentioned recommendations before!

When expecting their first child, humans grow into the role of parents, which causes insecurity. They must learn to handle their new roles. The feeling of insecurity will weaken in time and with more children to come, but it will never disappear completely. Insecurity on the parents' part is to be considered a positive indication of how much they care for their child.

Remember your first days in the children's group.
Could you understand the children's messages?
Could you grasp what the children were expecting from you?
How could you make yourself understood?
Were they strenuous first days?
How much time did you need for your preparations?

A wide scope of different consultants is available to the parents. They might be supportive or cause insecurity. Consultancy may be offered either in written form or by real people imposing themselves on the parents. Their advice might be cost-free, in vain, or for nothing. They may have the best of intentions, but what do they really achieve?

Do parents really need consultants?
Is it necessary for them to be instructed in parenthood?
Are teachers for parents really required?

In every society, the consultative roles were or still are traditionally taken by the elder family members, the relations, the sages and friends of either gender. Along with the break-up of these traditional social forms and increasing knowledge at the same time, other people (male or female) become consultants too, for instance paediatricians, psychologists, teachers, social workers and... childcare workers.

Within the guild of consulting supporters, the childcare workers' occupation is only one amongst many. This makes them – whether they like it or not – members of a phalanx against parental competence. From the mere existence of professional supporters the parents might conclude that they are threatened, that they 'alone won't make it'. It should be remembered that all professional supporters are eager to work and earn their living. Therefore they have to justify their existence. Consequently, most of them keep underlining their professional skills, thereby inevitably devaluing the parents' competences. Will these impressions lead to even more disturbance among the parents, or will they feel safer, knowing that they are being observed by a lot of people?

Parents who enter a childcare centre for the first time, either for collecting more information or for enrolling their child, have already been in touch with many professional experts long since. Were they adequately consulted, supported and given security? Presumably they will have been rather over- than under-consulted. Under the influence of their earlier experiences, they are now joining a childcare centre. They know that childcare workers are members of the system of professional consultants. Consequently, their first contacts will most probably not be free from reservations.

Further problems can arise, because the childcare workers as supporters and experts are not fully acknowledged (see also principle 2). In the hierarchical order of all social occupations they are positioned in the lower ranks, because childcare centres as a social form of education cannot everywhere be taken for granted, let alone be highly accepted, guaranteed, further developed or promoted. The range of reservations offers appropriate statements for each relevant situation:

- Members of extended-family oriented societies are grappling with questions such as: Is it acceptable that the child is cared for outside the family? Are people outside the family allowed insight and influence?

- In the 'western industrial countries' the questions will rather focus on the time spent or the beginning of childcare in the centre. To what extent may mothers (and fathers) pursue their job careers, so that it will still be to the child's benefit? How many hours is a child to be cared for in a centre? At which age shall a child go into day-care?

In every culture the reservations about children in day-care have become more or less public. They put parents under strain, either in form of pressure imposed by tradition or the findings of new research results. All the same, parents trust the childcare workers to take care of their children! Please remember that trust develops from experience. If parents send their child into day-care despite the generally known reservations about childcare centres, they simultaneously endow their child with anticipated confidence in the childcare worker. They may be cautious but by no means suspicious. What is more: they have the right and they are obliged to be attentive, otherwise they would lack parental responsibility.

It is now the childcare workers' turn to live up to the confidence placed upon them by providing the children as well as the parents with high-quality performance. They can try to 'counterbalance the account of trust' by returning the same anticipatory confidence to the parents. Each childcare worker can assume that parents wish to achieve the best possible for their child, even if they sometimes do not seem to meet the professional requirements.

2

PART TWO

basis for co-operation

Since safe ground cannot always be built on, other anchor points must be established.

The house is designed, important preconditions are settled. Constructing the foundation can get under way now. Is the house built on posts, will there be a cellar? Will it be made of brick, concrete or wood?

In a figurative sense, all these issues are left to your decision. Describing the manifold possibilities of putting them into practice would be too much to ask. Therefore I think that detailed (building) instructions are not as important for the childcare workers' activities as the fundamentals summarised in the following five principles. They deepen the discussion on the purpose and the assignment of early childhood support, because their definition will in advance decisively influence the relationship between childcare workers and parents. The five principles stir up the professional identity of the childcare workers, not for the sake of questioning it, but for testing its firmness. The professional competence of childcare workers is clearly respected by assigning them difficult tasks. At the same time, however, it is assumed that this competence cannot fully unfold without parental expertise.

Apart from the respect for the parents' (educational) expertise, which is to be integrated into professional early childhood support, there exists a second idea, linking the five following principles. I am trying to support *co-operation* by firstly analysing the childcare workers' and parents' independent fields of competence. It only seems as if this purposeful separation is contradictory to the goal. It is, however, based on the experience that *co-operation* will work above all with people provided with their own secured fields, which enable them to get into touch with others, if, whenever or to which extent they find it appropriate. Parents act on a voluntary basis. Childcare workers, as a rule, have no choice if they are interested in good quality childminding.

PRINCIPLE 6

1 2 3 4 5 6 7 8 9 10 11 12

Assume that most children, parents and childcare workers live in normal circumstances — at least according to the variety admitted by the society they live in and whatever this means in reality for the quality of daily life!

Not every society can afford childcare centres, since money and other resources need to be provided. A society must be quite wealthy and also convinced that childcare centres are institutions worth investing in for the future. Childcare centres exist where family life might be harmed but by no means destroyed. The institutions are available in such places where children spend the major part of the day within their families, but where additional education and care are needed. Generally, parents are at hand even when being in employment. Wherever people are in trouble, seeking refuge, or living in camps, neither childcare centres in the true sense, nor early childhood support can be found.

What is true of the society you live in?
There are places in childcare centres available for every fifth, third or almost any child.
Employed parents are more likely to be given a place for their child than others who find it desirable for pedagogical reasons.
The criteria of admission are adjusted to the people's neediness.

Some population groups cannot make use of the childcare centres' offers, because the places are too costly, people are discriminated, or the policies of the childcare centres do not correspond to their own educational goals.

Let us assume that most parents live according to the standards that are common, normal or generally accepted within their own society. We may now conclude that – apart from a few exceptions – the parents represent the range of possible childrearing practices as accepted by society. All of them might have different ideas. Possibly, they act against the advice and recommendations of professional consultants, but the majority of the parents raise their children according to common sense and common law. Therefore, they cannot be generally blamed for not caring for their children.

This principle takes some strain off the childcare workers and they can calm down. They need not live in permanent alert, because other people take charge of the children's well-being too – only in a different way.

The above-mentioned statements and the like can only generally be applied. They are meant to exemplify the basic concept. Apart from that, there exist exceptional situations which require the childcare workers' particular attention. Clearly, cases of child neglect or abuse must be quoted in this context. Each single case is one too many, but then again we should not be tempted to generalise or start activities due to a single detected offence.

There are children who lead a risky life, because the circumstances they were born into are far from being ideal. Childcare workers are quite familiar with such heightened risks. They are aware that these children are not offered the previously mentioned average living conditions and opportunities by their societies.

A final aspect takes a look at the situation of children whose parents, due to ethnical, religious, traditional or other reasons, have assimilated attitudes towards education and children's rights which are totally different from what is accepted by society – provided this has become commonly known. Take for example the circumcision of young women. With view to immigration, this could become threatening to quite a number of girls even in our (Western European) culture. In such cases and the like, the standards of parental education can by no means be tolerated, or to a limited extent only. Under such circumstances, children's individual rights as they are taken down in the Human Rights Act or in a state's constitution – for instance the right of physical well-being – have to be given priority and put into practice accordingly.

We may also conclude that (almost) all parents are doing the best possible for their child. There is no reason for undervaluing the parents' efforts and achievements. For our children, we ourselves may favour other values, prefer other goals and strive for more consistent methods of childrearing, but this does not necessarily mean that we are the better parents and/or childcare workers.

Given that parents, as a rule, stand for the range of socially accepted methods of childminding, their views are to be respected as common opinion within the respective society – at home and in the childcare centre. What parents require from day-care cannot be interpreted as coincidental individual opinions, but rather socially accepted expectations which childcare workers have to tackle.

PRINCIPLE

1 2 3 4 5 6
7 8 9 10 11 12

Take into consideration that professionals need the parents knowledge and expertise!

Each form of pedagogical interaction with children, however well-founded it may be, will not become efficient without the parents' consent. Parents have more than an intuitive understanding of education. Although it is certainly different from the professionals' view, it is not of minor importance. They are the people whom a child is first and usually most closely attached to. They are experts on their child, their own life's circumstances and their living conditions in general.

Can you agree to the following statements?
Parents are not the reason for arising problems.
In case of problems, the way to an appropriate solution can only be found via the parents, otherwise it will lead astray.

Education should not be considered an event in which children, regardless of their individuality, are faced with offers for improving their abilities and skills. In fact, children's individual interests, abilities and skills mark the outset of early childhood support. Knowing them as well as possible is an important precondition for further development. As a rule, childcare workers take care of a child for a limited part of the day only. They perceive the child exclusively within the special context of the *childcare centre*. They observe the child's activities and reactions within their self-created frame-work.

Only seldomly do they know whether the child behaves differently in other contexts and what skills he or she develops there.

Parents have known their child from his or her first day of existence. There is a lot that they would tell a childcare worker – if they were certain that their knowledge would be regarded a basis for pedagogical interaction. Parents are fond of contributing to their child's well-being and development as long as their ideas are not undervalued but integrated instead. Parents are willing to co-operate provided they can fulfil an important task.

Children benefit from the *co-operation* between childcare workers and parents, because it will spare them loyalty conflicts. Childcare workers profit from the parents' knowledge which helps them to broaden their basic information on the children and their living conditions. It enables them to plan well-foundedly and to react more distinctly. In other words, the quality of the pedagogical work improves and consequently society's acceptance of the childcare workers' performances.

Example 1: In Corby, England, the parents contribute essentially to the pedagogical offers of the childcare centre by writing down their observations of their child at home. The diary records are the main source of information on the child for the childcare workers. The parents – mostly mothers – find out which *scheme* their child is presently most interested in. This all takes place in an area where the majority of the residents are unemployed and have not completed school education.

Example 2: An everyday incident. A childcare worker did not succeed in bringing a child to sleep, although he or she was obviously tired. She did not know that the child at home – according to tradition – was rocked to sleep in a large cloth.

The purpose of the institution roughly outlines the range of possible activities (see principle 3). Within this framework childcare workers can make a choice. They can either renounce the parents' knowledge or use it for their own pedagogical work. Respecting the parents as experts on their children widens the basis for co-operation on the one hand. On the other hand, disputes are more likely to come up.

Accepting parents as experts means listening to them, taking their views seriously, backing them. Self-reliant parents are not welcomed everywhere. They are difficult to handle, cause trouble, can in fact intimidate many a professional. Not every childcare worker and institutional body consider such parents an attractive perspective. As a matter of fact, some conflicts between parents and childcare workers only show, when parents are courageous enough to utter their view-points, wishes, and ideas. However, I am convinced that the parents' power will not generate new conflicts, but only reveal those already existing, which – finally – can be tackled together.

Avoiding the parents' involvement and power on the other hand seems the easier way of handling them. But remember how much energy it costs to suppress disputes and conflicts. Remember that disputes do not necessarily mean conflicts and that disputes can well lead to further personal development as well as more nearness among the people involved – this is true even of conflicts.

Example: Quality criteria for childcare centres from Birmingham (England):
Is the parents' expertise given a hearing, is it respected and appreciated?
Are the family background and the language respected and accepted?
Are the parents and their views on the childcare centre listened to?

Occasionally childcare workers fear that their professional prestige will suffer if parents are accepted as educational experts. I don't believe that this assumption is true. Certainly it is a question of how this expertise is defined by the childcare workers or which criteria it is measured by respectively. Should the standards be set by physicians, teachers or psychologists whose professionalism does not allow any interference from the outside? Consequently, each institution or responsible body will have to clarify whether parents should really be considered *outside observers* in early childhood support.
But do the just quoted examples really offer an appropriate orientation to the childcare workers? They don't, because the childcare workers' professionalism requires competent involvement on the parents' part. The quality of pedagogical professionalism does not only show in dealing with the children, but becomes evident in the *co-operation* and confrontation with the parents, too.

Even among physicians, first signs of rethinking could be observed over the past years. In the meantime, they have learnt that diseases are easier to analyse if patients are allowed active involvement. Also, they have realised that most indispositions include psychological components. A patient's recovery depends to a large extent on his or her personal activation.

PRINCIPLE 1 2 3 4 5 6 7 8 9 10 11 12

Childcare workers have to explain their work — parents do not need to justify their actions!

The eighth principle is explained within two contexts, firstly with respect to the priorities in education and secondly with respect to the question which of them may serve as a basis for the co-operation between childcare workers and parents.

Do you agree?
No children without parents.
No childcare centres without children.
No work places for childcare workers without children.
Childcare workers are paid for passing on information to parents and children.

Most countries protect the educational rights of parents, this in particular against intervention by the state authorities. However, once the children have reached a certain age, almost any state will claim its own right on the children. School education will then become compulsory.

As far as I know, no regulation can anywhere be found which makes participation in early childhood support compulsory for children at pre-school age. According to the UN-Convention on children's rights, it is agreed world wide that the upbringing and development of children before school age lies in the parents' responsibility. They are the only ones to decide how to manage their responsibility. Perhaps they will favour additional care and education programmes outside their families? All the same, early childhood support is not exclusively a private matter anymore. In many countries, childcare centres are considered an important linking element within the educational system. Governmental funds are made available in those countries where it is also in the society's interest that children make use of these additional offers.

Parents are reserved the sole rights on their child if they send him or her into day-care – and also during the time he or she is looked after by a childcare worker. They may expect to receive sufficient information about their child, their common goals, their development, daily experiences, food supply, well-being and much more. Otherwise they will not be able to pursue their rights adequately.

If childcare workers respond to the parents' right of information, we may roughly state that they meet the legal requirements and act correctly according to professional and civil understanding. However important this formal aspect of the right of information is for the parents, which, in return, explains the childcare worker's duty of information, the more it resembles a mere business arrangement and the less inspiring effect it may have on everyday practice. Hence, it may be of greater importance to the childcare workers that a well-functioning information flow is a precondition for the expected success. Positive results, satisfactory feedback, new ideas and eventful practice will be possible if childcare workers share their knowledge. Well instructed parents will sooner or later offer their information in return. Thus a childcare worker's basis and range of activities are extended (see principle 7), and the quality of the pedagogical work improves.

About Information

In juridical terminology, 'information' can be compared to 'a debt to be discharged at creditor's domicile'. That is to say: A person provided with essential information is obliged to convey it to others unasked. A potential recipient cannot be expected to continuously enquire for more, important information.

Information must be easy to understand. The corresponding standard is set by the recipient!

The information flow from the sender (under obligation) to the recipient (entitled) presents the minimal form of co-operation, followed by mutual information as its next stage of development. To put it more radically: if nothing else gets under way, at least the information flow must be safeguarded.

Almost all parents are interested in their children's well-being. They do not want to be excluded from their children's experiences during those hours when they themselves are not at hand. Parents are concerned and emotionally involved. Activating this involvement becomes a crucial aspect. Therefore it is necessary that parents receive information before their child is admitted to day-care. The *co-operation* with parents begins as soon as the institution makes information available to them – if and whenever they themselves desire it. Generally though, good quality early childhood support aims at detailed discourse with the parents, trying to avoid interview-resembling situations with professional questioners on the one side and those having to answer on the other side.

The *co-operation* between childcare workers and parents will have reached an advanced level, once the two sides are able to actually exchange information. The information provided by the parents puts the childcare worker under legal as well as professional obligation. Parents, though, are only bound to the childcare worker's information as long as the basic care for their child is concerned. Just to quote some examples: who is allowed to pick up the child, has the child got a temperature, is he or she allowed to swim or suffering from allergies?

In all other cases, the childcare worker may consider each single piece of parental information a sign of confidence.

I have been writing about the parents now for quite a while. Who are they really? What do they wish? What do they need? Which details from their lives are they willing to confide to the childcare worker. Which details do they find necessary to convey? Are they interested in supporting their child's education? Do they themselves hope for help? Do they expect it from the childcare worker or do they, purposefully, consult totally different agencies of support, therefore kindly and self-confidently rejecting any other offer, or do they evade this issue conscience-stricken?

Childcare workers and parents need a lot of basic information on each other before an exchange of intense, often confidential information can take place. Information channels and opportunities must be arranged for by the childcare worker. The process is getting under way, when she is about to make her work transparent. It is likely to continue if the parents' expectations and comments concerning the pedagogical work are explicitly welcomed.

PRINCIPLE 1 2 3 4 5 6 7 8 9 10 11 12

Take into account that vague agreements and/ or serious reasons might be at the root of the parents reactions if something goes wrong — they neither wish to disappoint nor insult you!

Misunderstandings happen, even with close friends. Also long-standing partners sometimes fail to reach to clearly defined agreements. Despite good intentions, a lot may go wrong. It is simply not enough that both sides *want* to achieve something together. Co-operation is complicated and susceptible to mistakes.

Do the following sentences sound familiar to you?
Although we did show much effort, only a few parents came!
It is always the same parents who make use of it!
Those who would really be needing it, do not want to be addressed anyway!
Although we have talked it over with each single mother beforehand, there were only so few cakes, helpers, and so little interest!

This principle shows in two variations. First possibility: childcare workers develop a number of ideas about what to offer to the parents and are disappointed if they do not make use of it. Second possibility: childcare workers wish for closer *co-operation* with the parents and expect them to become actively involved in the institution.

Variation 1

Let us assume that members of a childcare centre's staff have noticed that there are neither toys nor picture-books available in some of the children's homes. There may be several reasons for it: low family budget, the parents' conviction that children at that age do not really need them, other priorities on the parents' part and what have you... The staff develop a concept for a toy library and put it into practice stepwise. As a short term activity, the team calls in a parents' assembly on the topic 'toys and books in early childhood' and also invites a well-known lecturer. For the parents' support, the childcare workers organise an aftercare service. Thus the parents can go out in the evenings, they need not bother finding babysitters or worrying whether they will handle their child with sufficient sense of responsibility. A totally different kind of innovation, a parents' corner, is arranged for, where water, tea and coffee are offered to those parents who arrive at the centre after a day's work, punctually but exhausted .

Despite all efforts and good intentions, childcare workers learn that their additional services are not as demanded as they had hoped for. Perhaps they are not really necessary. Parents, on being asked about their personal viewpoints, might have considered it an attractive idea, but were not content enough with its realisation, the point of time, the expenses or the expenditure. They might have found their own solutions. They prefer drinking their coffee at home, once they have recovered from stressful shopping and can relax.

This leaves the childcare workers at a loss and they react disappointedly on the parents and their presumable lack of interest.

At the same time, this situation may lead to amazement and disappointment also on the parents' part. Can't childcare workers think of anything else than simply planning additional services? Is this what a childcare centre is good for? Aren't there... Children should always come in the first place! Childcare workers had better devote their time and energy to the children.

Variation 2

Childcare workers encourage parents to participate in the jubilee celebrations of the institution. They unmistakably signal to them that baking cakes, preparing salads or the like are appreciated as indications of sound co-operation. It does not need a festivity though. Through the childcare workers, the parents will understand that their practical work can be a possibility of contributing to the well-being of their children in the institution. For instance, they can present ('suggest') their ideas such as renovating the group room or cleaning the sandpit.

Does this imply that they could prove *good parents* if they actively participate? Who do they need to give evidence to? Actually, I do not intend to carry this example too far. Problems will arise earlier, that is, if parents' contributions are reduced to acting according to the childcare workers' wishes and likings. The situation will become difficult if the parents' contributions are limited to assisting and fulfilling requirements within a set frame. Is it not understandable that under such circumstances only a few and 'always the same' parents will become involved? It would not be surprising if the childcare workers' reactions changed from asking the parents to appealing to them: 'Frankly, we do expect more people to turn up next time!' Provided this situation occurs a second time, disappointment will soon spread again: 'It's no use trying again anyway; parents are simply not interested.'

If childcare workers did not feel insulted in such situations, but considered them a result of mutual misunderstandings – that is to say, literally having a wrong understanding of each other – they would be able to recognise the true reasons behind them. Let me quote three examples which will help to explain the above stated situation. In my opinion, they offer plausible reasons for what is going on:

1. The childcare workers are mistaking the parents' current living conditions. Possibly, the parents have been asked for help all too often. As a rule, they have to meet further obligations outside the institution. If they refrain from participating or contributing respectively, they protect themselves against too much strain – also with respect to their families' welfare.

2. The childcare workers have initiated the festivity and planned it perfectly. Parents are allowed to fill the intended gaps with their contributions. However, there is no room for their own creativity. In that case, parents may feel used and refrain from participating.

3. The childcare workers failed to see that they had actually requested the parents' assistance. It is in the nature of requests that they can be rejected unpunished. What is more: help does not have anything to do with really important work. Assistance even less so. It is additional support and is virtually unnecessary. Parents therefore may feel underestimated in their competences and consequently stay away.

If the true circumstances are not critically examined, there is hardly any chance for a better future co-operation between the childcare workers and the parents.

This situation could possibly lead to amazement and disappointment also on the parents' part. They might think:

- After all, we are paying for it, so why should we do extra work?
- Actually we are paying so that others are working.
- So far so good, but these efforts should rather be devoted to the children.
- I do not think that I can live up to the childcare workers' expectations.
- What the childcare workers are up to is absolutely silly.
- If they had asked me whether I would like to take charge of..., I would have agreed.
- Did I get it right that I cannot participate without contributing?
- I don't think I should really go there if I do not contribute. I find this simply too embarrassing.
- Why can't the childcare workers for once seek the kind of support that I am able to offer?

PRINCIPLE 1 2 3 4 5 6 7 8 9 10 11 12

Discuss competences and resources — not deficits!

At the end of the ninth principle I had an imaginary parent ask: 'Why can't the childcare worker for once seek the kind of support that I am able to offer?' It alluded to the unsatisfactory situation that despite the childcare workers' wish for parental *co-operation* and the parents' explicit will to *contribute*, they still do not meet. The tenth principle offers a further explanatory model.

Clarification becomes necessary again!
Childcare workers and parents talk at cross-purposes if the one side is asking for *assistance* whereas the other is talking of *contribution*.
They use different wording and show different expectations towards each other.
Childcare workers are interested in getting something additional (assistance) from the parents – what are they themselves willing to additionally give in return?
Parents want to become active – is each single contribution equally appreciated?
Is *assistance* identical to *co-operation*?

A symptomatic example: the childcare workers have planned 'something pleasant and important' – possibly a party or game-activities –, wishing for the parents' *co-operation* so that their idea can be realised. However, if the parents do not join in, typical reactions such as disappointment or annoyance will arise.

What might have happened? Things do not always run smoothly (see principle 9). The childcare workers have failed to make a clear distinction between their wish for and their appeal to parental co-operation. Or they did not notice that they had arranged the situation similar to their pedagogical work.

The pedagogical offers for the children show what is actually going on. A long time before, the childcare worker has prepared an 'important and pleasant activity' which is now to be carried out by the children's group. Anticipating the children's opposition, the pedagogical staff are aware that children must be motivated first. After all, they are expected to learn or respectively practise something in order to tackle the next step towards improving their competences. This is possible to a limited extent only, because children learn above all what they really want to and not what is expected from them. They will become actively involved if they are given the chance of modifying the offers available and are not limited to imitating, executing and assisting.

What is difficult to realise with the children cannot be motivating for parents either. The weak response to *assistance* should not come as a surprise, because it is merely execution that is asked for. With such methods, childcare workers are running a great risk, because nobody is fond of merely carrying out what others have worked out for him or her.

- Nobody wants to be restricted to subordinate services. It is considered unworthy.

- Nobody is content with simply colouring the childcare workers' ready-made sketches. It is regarded boring.
- Nobody wants to be reminded of his or her feeling of dependency in typical class-room situations. It is perceived as unpleasant.

Parents refrain from such situations, because they do not seek a confrontation with those childcare workers whose efforts they basically acknowledge. They do not wish to become the target group of pedagogically intended activities. They are interested in sharing their children's lives and in shaping their future. Whoever is able to make use of his or her skills, because they are really required, will not have to be motivated additionally.

Parents will contribute to the extent that they find appropriate for the set frame. If they are eager to participate, making out gaps ('What do we need?') to be filled by the parents should be avoided. Parents should rather be asked about their ideas. What stimulating ideas can they think of?

Afterwards the suggestions are revised together and decision making focuses on (the sequence of) their realisation. Parents are given the opportunity and support to put their contributions into practice.

Childcare workers can rely on the parents' ideas and skills. There are more available than may be thought of at first sight. Parents are provided with an abundance of competences which they apply at home, in clubs, in citizens' initiatives or in their jobs. How many of these skills are activated in the childcare centre?

Example: In a programme for the organisational development of childcare centres ('Step by Step') it says: Each single parent is able to teach something!

Given that parents are both, addressees of the childcare workers' pedagogical programmes and their children's teachers at the same time, it follows that even childcare workers can learn from the parents.

This view modifies the common attitude towards the childcare workers' professionalism. This attitude, acquired during their professional training, can now and then become completely reversed, because they return to the status of learners. When elaborating on the fourth and fifth principle, I questioned the job profile of the unimpeachable childminder. In my opinion, this profession is not defined by its exclusiveness, but rather by the competence to co-operate with others and to get ahead jointly. It becomes necessary to adopt the varying roles of both teacher and learner, because this way the parents' competences will be acknowledged on an equal basis and the culture of *co-operation* can be perceived as a matter of give and take.

The principle of discussing competences and resources will positively affect the regular conversations with parents about their child. As a rule, a childcare worker can make parents avoid such meetings by instilling the fear that the child's developmental and behavioural deficits will become the subject of discussion. Nobody is keen on hearing unpleasant news. Of course, this does not mean tabooing serious harm to the children's development – because then necessary support would be denied. However, this situation does not apply to the majority of the children.

Deviant behaviour (of the children) in the childcare centre is often seen as a deficit in behaviour which the parents are to be blamed for. In my view, however, it is rather the question of additional patterns of behaviour – why else should they be suppressed? Besides, I think that the problem of rule offence – this is what deviant behaviour is mostly associated with – is to be solved by the childcare worker and the child exclusively. Parents should not be bothered with it. Tattling childcare workers do not achieve anything at all. Hoping that the parents will take influence on their child at home, the childcare workers do not realise that they are about to lose their educational competence. The child notices his or her childcare worker's helplessness and will (continue to) show different forms of behaviour in the home-setting and at the childcare centre. In the beginning, his or her parents might be surprised at the childcare worker's reports, because these problems are simply unknown to them. Gradually they will realise that they are asked to undertake *corrections*. In other words: the parents recognise that the blame is actually put on them. Each presumable deficit of a child that the childcare worker reports to the parents has the effect of hidden accusation or of assessing guilt respectively. Do the parents have other choices but to resist or refrain?

Example:
Rule No. 9 (in a total number of 26) from a childcare centre:
If you spank, kick, beat or attack another child, you will be given a warning. If this happens once more, your behaviour will be reported to your parents.

If this tenth principle is seriously taken into consideration, childcare workers and parents will find a lot to talk about. The childcare workers learn about the child in situations different from the home setting and for the major part of the day. Parents can share their child's life, even when they are not at hand, by talking about his or her interests, activities and experiences. If the conversation turns to the child's stages of development, comparisons with other children, or statistical surveys providing average data, should be avoided, because they may underline the shortcomings of the relevant child and emphasise the other children's progress. However, this does not really matter. It is of vital importance which competences a child is provided with, which stage of development he or she has reached, which step could be taken next and how it might be supported by everybody involved.

3

PART THREE

ensuring co-operation

There is no security, only various forms of insecurity.

The prerequisites for house building are settled, the foundations are laid. The walls are being erected – but not at this point. The practical conversion of the principles, that is stepwise applying and further developing them, is left to you. In conclusion, I will offer two additional principles in two new, short chapters instead. Each building needs to be secured from the very outset throughout each new single phase. Once accomplished, attentive maintenance – now and then even an overall renovation – will secure the achievements. Positioning the securing principles at the end of the written sequence of principles may therefore be misleading. The two final principles can become effective anytime.

The first principle comprises more than the *co-operation* between childcare workers and parents and does in fact finally lead to the subject of *partnership*. I would like to point out once more that *partnership* can develop along with the quality of *co-operation*. No matter how these two terms are defined, it is of crucial importance that the appropriate rights are continuously generated, observed and ensured.

The second principle for ensuring *co-operation* emphasises once again the childcare worker's outstanding role. However strongly the institutional circumstances, the job assignment and the legal framework may influence *co-operation*, it is for the childcare worker to decide in everyday practice whether parents will be blamed for arising problems or whether she will search for other reasons.

PRINCIPLE 1 2 3 4 5 6 7 8 9 10 11 12

Ensuring partnership means granting equal rights to all people involved.

This principle differs from the others. It is not phrased as an appeal to the childcare workers and their activities but as a statement. It can be considered a precondition. This principle does not refer to *co-operation* but to real *partnership*. All the same, it is appropriate at this point, because it helps to understand the approach.

Even the following conclusions are acceptable:
In order to achieve *partnership*, equal rights must be granted to all people involved.- Striving for *partnership* only makes sense if all participants are granted equal rights.

With this alteration I am trying to underline the difference to the former principles whose application depends first of all on their acceptance by the team of the childcare workers. This eleventh principle rather - but not exclusively - depends on the body's general conditions and the societal as well as legal potentialities. Whether parents are entitled participation, can hardly be decided by one institution alone. This makes initiating and ensuring *partnership* a difficult task, especially if the body is targeting other goals, or if this form of co-operation with the parents is totally unusual and new to a society.

Those in favour of *co-operation* and even *partnership* with the parents should neither give up hope nor content themselves with waiting for the preconditions to change. On the contrary, the societal idea of *partnership* needs room to gradually grow. Its introduction must be developed step by step. Opposition and setbacks will have to be faced. The higher the degree of consent about the goal (see principle 1) and the clearer the respectively achieved level is to all people involved, the fewer the failures that may occur.

For the pre-stages of *partnership*, the principle can also read as follows:
For each form of *co-operation* the appropriate rights of involvement and participation must be generated.

Co-operation can be realised in many variations and at different degrees of intensity. The parents' rights of involvement and participation must suit the requested intensity of *co-operation*. Too small a frame will cause disappointment; too large a frame leads to unrealisable expectations.

Any institution is suitable for getting this project under way. However, *co-operation* is not only important in its abstract meaning. From the very outset, parents (and childcare workers) need to practically learn that participation is worth the necessary effort. Thus success, or at least the fun of joining in, form the ideal basis for becoming involved.
Effort and commitment will pay if *co-operation* is wanted not only for a limited period of time, but if the integration of the parents, their ideas and competences have become part of the childcare centre's *culture*. Such a culture of participation outwardly shows in regularity and control (for example by safeguarding it in writing). The desired degree of parental involvement can also be concluded from the topics and the contents these rights are covering. Thus the abovementioned statement that the parents' rights need to fit the

desired intensity of *co-operation* also reads as follows: the rights of involvement and participation as really granted to the parents reflect the desired intensity of *co-operation*.

Example: In Reggio Emilia, communal crèches and nurseries are run by so-called parents' committees. With each committee, parents constitute half of the members, the other 50% consist of childminders, consultants and even neighbours. All of them decide on the budget, recruit new staff members, are integrated in the pedagogical planning process etc.

Such far-reaching parental rights help to establish a framework of responsibility suited to the targeted *partnership*. They serve as a basis for articulating real interests and participating with real responsibility – not in the moral but in the legal meaning of the word. Creating a solid footing for co-operation means that the formal rights must be known to all parents. They must offer easy access to the institution and bring about benefit to all people involved.

Each childcare worker may grapple with the following questions:

- What rights are parents being granted in our institution?
- Are parents permitted access anytime?
- Do the parents' formal rights on their children inside our organisation restrict their legal rights outside?
- Do parents enjoy their rights in the true sense of the word or are they merely allowed participation in virtually never-ending board meetings?
- Is there an information and decision making scheme for the essential issues of the institution in which parents are integrated?

The answers will show whether the *co-operation* between childcare workers and parents is supported and how much conformity there is between the demands and reality. It will become obvious which of the two items requires modification.

PRINCIPLE 1 2 3 4 5 6 7 8 9 10 11 12

First of all look for reasons within the institution or the organisational context if parents do not co-operate!

This publication addresses practitioners in childcare centres. In this context, they represent my target group for improving *co-operation* with the parents. I assume that the professionals are more likely to become activated (*anticipated demand for activation*), that is to say that, in case of doubt, they will have to take the initiative for getting *co-operation* under way.

Through her activities, each childcare worker can directly influence the parents. On the other hand, it is up to her whether she prefers staying in the background, collecting the parents' impulses. Also, she can organise the setting and the time in order to promote the parents' activities. Additionally, she may call on the institutional body for changing the general conditions.

If you want others to change, start changing yourself first.

I stated above that the childcare worker is to play an active role in the *co-operation* with the parents. This assumption is essentially based on the idea that she is generally provided with the necessary competences and that, let alone the children, she will probably profit most from *co-operation*.

Although *anticipated demand for activation* does not mean that the childcare worker is entirely in charge of everything at stake, positive or negative results included, there is no getting around that she is responsible for finding the appropriate ways and means leading to *co-operation*. Her responsibility does not end when failures occur.

On the contrary, I would like to explicitly add. If long-standing routine or new initiatives do not result in satisfactory outcomes for the *co-operation* between childcare workers and parents (anymore), the childcare worker will have to ask why. The following simple answers are possible:

- We do not need it any longer anyway, soon there will be new children and parents coming to our centre!
- As usual, parents cannot be bothered!
- Earlier, parents used to be less demanding!

These answers do not help to intensify *co-operation*. Apart from being absolutely useless, these exaggerated examples share a further common element. They are mentally focusing on the parents who would only need to behave *somewhat different* to make efforts for *co-operation* a more rewarding issue. Against this approach I will now oppose this final principle.

Unless parents are willing to *co-operate* such as hoped for by the childcare worker, the reasons may be directly rooted in her work or respectively her style of approaching the task. It goes without saying that the childcare worker would first of all have to critically reassess her work.

It seems as if other components become effective in this context. Identifying and analysing them is an important precondition for further rewarding efforts. What about the outer framework? Does the scheduling allow the parents' participation? Is your institution pursuing totally unusual goals?

Are you applying innovative, but unaccustomed methods? Are the formal rights made to fit your idea of *co-operation*?

This final chapter is a supplement to the ninth principle. If parents do not become involved, you had better ask what is keeping them off instead of giving up or behaving reproachfully. Parents do not generally refuse involvement but have their reasons for acting either way. There is no use of blaming the parents for lacking *co-operation*. Although this appears the easiest way of tracing the difficulties, it will not offer you further-reaching explanations or even problem-solving strategies.

Colophon

Twelve principles
for a successful co-operation between childcare workers
and parents
Roger Prott & Annette Hautumm

ISBN 90 6665 618 2
NUR 742

Editor
Krijn Peter Hesselink

Design cover
Lieve Maas, Uitgeverij SWP

Layout and typesetting
Redactiebureau Ron Heijer, Markelo

Publisher
Dennis H. van Santen

For information on other SWP Publications:
P.O.Box 257, 1000 AG Amsterdam
Tel.: + 31 (0)20 330 72 00
E-mail: swp@swpbook.com
Internet: www.swpbook.com